THE BUZZ

A play by Lydia Rynne

The Bread & Roses Theatre
68 Clapham Manor Street
London SW4 6DZ
www.breadandrosestheatre.co.uk

© Lydia Rynne

First published by The Bread & Roses Theatre in 2018.

Lydia Rynne has asserted her right to be identified as the author of this work. All rights reserved. Requests to reproduce the text in whole or in part should be addressed to the publisher.

Cover photography: Velenzia Spearpoint
Cover model: Sassy Clyde
Design/Formatting: Tessa Hart

ISBN 978-1-912504-04-6

Amateur and Professional Performing Rights

No performance of any kind of this play may be given unless a licence has been obtained, including excerpts and readings. Application should be made before rehearsals begin. Publication of these plays does not indicate availability for performance. This applies to all mediums and all languages.
To enquire about availability for performing rights and the necessary steps to undertake to obtain a licence, please contact info@breadandrosestheatre.co.uk in the first instance.

Lydia Rynne
Lydia is a writer for stage and screen. A finalist in BFI/Creative England's Funny Girls scheme, Lydia penned the short film Nugget Love which was selected as a Sundance Ignite Finalist. Her one woman play Hear Me Howl premiered in London in March 2018 and went on to the Plymouth and Edinburgh fringe festivals in Summer 2018.

THE BUZZ - *A play by Lydia Rynne*

The Buzz was first performed at The Bread & Roses Theatre from 8th to 19th May 2018, after coming top 3 in The Bread & Roses Playwriting Award 2016/2017. *It was presented with the following cast and creatives:*

CAST

Kyla
Sassy Clyde

Josh
Andy Umerah

Nate
Gabriel Cagan

Anon
Hannah Duffy

CREATIVES

Director
Velenzia Spearpoint

Set & Costume Designer
Sally Hardcastle

Sound & Lighting Designer
Chuma Emembolu

Assistant Director
Gwenan Bain

Movement Director
Roman Berry

Producing Company
The Bread & Roses Theatre Company (BRTC)

Producer
Ella Gamble

Creative Producers
Rebecca Pryle & Tessa Hart

Assistant Producer
Stephanie Hartland

*Note: This script went to print before the end of rehearsals and may vary slightly from that presented on stage.

THE BUZZ - *A play by Lydia Rynne*

Characters
Kyla - 33 years old.
Josh - 28. Boyfriend of Kyla.
Nate - 26. Kyla's brother.
Anon - 24. Friends with Nate.

THE BUZZ - *A play by Lydia Rynne*

Early hours of the morning. The open plan kitchen-lounge of a luxury London penthouse. On a glass coffee table, there is an open laptop. The TV plays a celebrity gossip channel that we can barely make out but can be continuous throughout.
Voices off. The door to the flat swings open and KYLA and JOSH enter, KYLA mid-rant.

KYLA — and I'm like, I get it, you're happy, but you've got a thousand other people here most of them wanting to get on with winning slash losing their awards and a million more people watching at home waiting for an ad break to go fetch their shepherd's pie out the microwave -

Josh simultaneously scans the laptop, his phone, and glances up at the TV, while KYLA chucks her belongings aside and searches the kitchen cupboards.

KYLA -and you know what? No-one actually cares about your first lesbian kiss that inspired your fourth album - where's my wine? I had half a bottle of red -

Kyla stands in front of the TV, blocking Josh's view. He gives up trying to look past her and returns his attention to the laptop instead.

KYLA You know they gave it to Justin Bieber last year, the Lifetime Achievement Award? Lifetime achievement in what?! Being a cunt?

Josh isn't listening so Kyla tries again.

KYLA Your speech wasn't so bad tonight Josh...

JOSH Not this again..

KYLA I'm serious - bold yet bashful, funny yet poignant. Like the best ever best man speech at the best wedding ever.

JOSH Babe, you know how long that list of names was.

KYLA Thirty four - I counted.

THE BUZZ - *A play by Lydia Rynne*

JOSH   And you know what Bobby and KJ are like -

KYLA   They pretty much blank me, so not really.

JOSH   It was a big night for everyone -

KYLA   Everyone in the whole world! In the whole universe!

JOSH   KJ actually said before I went up, he said 'you forget one of these guys names, they'll make sure you're history by the end of the month', and then something about squeezing my balls into a test tube and stamping on the test tube -

KYLA   When's this happening? I want front row seats.

JOSH   Kyla baby, you know I couldn't have made this album without you.

KYLA   But they don't know that do they? Most of them lot - the people that matter - they don't even know who I am anymore!

JOSH   Who cares?! Being known is bullshit. All I want to do is make music. And you - you keep me grounded.

He runs his fingers down her body, letting his hands rest on her breasts.

JOSH   Particularly these guys.

He clears his throat, as if preparing to make a speech.

JOSH   I'd like to thank Trixie and Delilah, for being there for me, through thick and thin -

KYLA   Thelma and Louise actually, they're feminist tits!

JOSH   I don't know where I'd be without you two. Probably alone, on a bed of money, forever scouring Pornhub to find your identical twins.

She gives in - and kisses him. A phone bleep - Josh pulls away immediately, sits back up, looking at his phone screen.

JOSH   The red carpet shots have come through.

KYLA   And? How do we look?

JOSH   There's not much up yet... Let's go to bed yeah?

She watches him for a moment, suspicious, before grabbing the phone from his hands - she looks hurt but covers it up with bravado, quickly.

KYLA   Wow Josh! You look... I mean you are WORKING that carpet

JOSH   Not all the coverage will be up, always takes a few hours you know that -

KYLA   No that is a keeper. Hey we should get it blown up!

JOSH   Kyla, baby -

KYLA   I mean, what an elbow. Hel-lo Of all the elbows that've been lucky enough to get photographed next to The Joshua Franklyn, I'd say mine's up there with the best of 'em...

JOSH   You're funny.

KYLA   Shame they didn't get at least the hem of my dress in what with how long I spent finding the perfect hue to match your eyes, just like you asked.. Do you think my old presenting agent will get back in touch now? Hey maybe I could get into elbow modelling, what do you think? And the award for Best newcomer, Goes to .... Kyla's Elbow.

Kyla makes her elbow bow as Josh shakes his head at her, but smiles, plays along, clapping. Kyla pretends to take an award and ventriloquists for her elbow, like it's her puppet.

THE BUZZ - A play by Lydia Rynne

KYLA   Thank you, thanks guys, wow.... First off, I'd like to thank my agent, Kyla, you always believed in me... also my identical twin and understudy who lives opposite, of course my sponsors the amazing Dove moisturiser, and my all time favourite band, Elbow, who apparently named themselves after me!?! Love you guys!!

Josh feigns upset.

JOSH   You didn't thank me.

KYLA   Guess now you know how it feels.

Josh gets another phone alert and stands, eyes on his phone as he makes his way towards the bedroom.

KYLA   Where are you going?

JOSH   Got that shoot tomorrow, need my beauty sleep. You did well tonight.

KYLA   I did try not to have too much fun, like you asked.

JOSH   You're taking the piss but you know, with my US tour coming up KJ says it's important that everything else, like my private life and stuff -

KYLA   I.e. don't let me go on a bender with my mates and get papped dancing in Walkabout to Dr Dre?

JOSH   What? No - they didn't mention that. But why were you in Walkabout?

KYLA   Don't worry, I won't be going back anytime soon. They don't invite me out anymore. Turns out they prefer not to get photographed when they're trying to let their hair down on a saturday night.

JOSH   Point is, my private life just needs to stay... uncomplicated. Clean.

Kyla makes a snoring noise.

KYLA	One time complications sold records. Look at Fleetwood Mac, you really think they'd have been as massive if they were celibate and sober?
JOSH	It was easier back then. All they had to do was turn up and play the music. There's loads more pressure on artists these days, all this social media shit -
KYLA	Artist. Strange word that.
JOSH	You're angling for a fight and I'm too tired -
KYLA	I'm not, I'm just saying, you used to come home and reach for the guitar, now it's gathering dust while you reach for the laptop instead.

Josh doesn't want to rise to it, turns and heads towards the bedroom again.

KYLA	So you admit it?
JOSH	Admit what.
KYLA	That you've sold out.
JOSH	I don't like you when you're pissed.
KYLA	But we're always pissed.
JOSH	*I'm* not.
KYLA	Liar.
JOSH	Had one glass of Prosecco, the one they gave out at the door.
KYLA	And all the wine at the table -
JOSH	Didn't touch it. You did, saw you.
KYLA	You were watching me?!

THE BUZZ - A play by Lydia Rynne

JOSH   You were making quite a show of it Kyla - was more wine on the table than in the glass by the interval.

KYLA   I was HAPPY.

JOSH   What about?

KYLA   For YOU. For you and your fucking award!?! Jesus!

JOSH   Awards

KYLA   Clapping away, and maybe some wine may have been in the vicinity, and suffered a blow... But don't worry about it. Maybe I won't applaud next time. Just sit there demurely sipping on sparkling water like the rest of the skinny rats. I'm talking about your lot's girlfriends...

JOSH   I guessed that Kyla

KYLA   I mean, what are KJ and Bobby doing going out with teenagers -

JOSH   Maybe cos those girls look like they're enjoying themselves, maybe cos they're grateful for the opportunity?

KYLA   No teenager wants to bang a sixty plus rhino Josh... They're obviously hoping for a break or something.

JOSH   And that bothers you because?

KYLA   I find it creepy. Pathetic. There's a stench of... desperation... Like how I imagine child beauty pageants smell...

Josh leaves.

KYLA   Like they've been doused in, I dunno... Cherry Soda

Josh re-enters.

JOSH   Say that again.

KYLA   You what?

JOSH   They smell like - ?

KYLA   Like a child beauty?

JOSH   Like Cherry Soda... That's good.

He grabs the laptop, snaps the lid open, sits on the sofa again and starts typing furiously.

JOSH   She... smells... like... Cherry Soda... That's seriously hot -

KYLA   It's supposed to be derogatory...

Josh holds a finger up to silence her, as he continues typing.

KYLA   So did you - did you manage to speak to KJ in the end?

JOSH   'She tries to hide her hotness, but she... she...

KYLA   Grew up in Totnes?

Josh goes to type this.

KYLA   That was a joke. Don't write that. So, did you?

JOSH   Hmmm?

KYLA   Only cos you said tonight might be a good time, everyone on a high and all that?

Nothing from Josh

THE BUZZ - *A play by Lydia Rynne*

KYLA	You know the more I've been thinking about it the more it feels like the timing couldn't be better. The third album, isn't that when they all start branching out? The Beatles started taking LSD, Fleetwood Mac started not sleeping with each other. I mean it's almost like we're a team anyway, you with the melody, me with the words? Josh?

JOSH shuts his laptop and looks up.

JOSH	What's that baby?
KYLA	Us..Us making an album together.
JOSH	Yeah definitely.
KYLA	So you spoke to them?
JOSH	Who?
KYLA	KJ and his people - the people you said you had to speak to?
JOSH	Yeah I mentioned it, yeah. She smells like Cherry Soda. I fucking love that.

He grabs her and kisses her with force, then puts the laptop away again and stands.

KYLA	Wait, so you actually told them?
JOSH	Kyla if I say I'm going to do something, I do it.
KYLA	And?
JOSH	They're proper keen.
KYLA	Seriously?
JOSH	Uhuh, it's totally in the pipeline.
KYLA	And how long is that pipe?

THE BUZZ - *A play by Lydia Rynne*

Josh laughs as if she's told a joke, pecks her on the top of her head then is distracted by something on the TV.

JOSH   Look at him, he's not sorry. He's just sorry he got *caught*!

KYLA   How do you know?

JOSH   Well it's obvious, why should he feel bad about girls throwing themselves at him?

KYLA   Are you fucking serious?! Why the hell would anyone throw themselves at THAT?! I'd rather throw myself, mouth wide open, into a river of shit. It's messed up!

Josh starts laughing.

KYLA   What?

JOSH   I was kidding! I knew that would rattle that rusty old feminist cage of yours.

KYLA   I actually believed you..

JOSH   I'm a pretty good actor right?

KYLA   You mean *liar*!

JOSH   KJ said some Hollywood producer wants to meet with me, about acting in something.

KYLA   You are joking?

JOSH   I'm serious. He obviously sees potential..

KYLA   What's wrong with just being one thing?! Everyone these days wants a finger in every fucking pie. What about your music?

JOSH   Yeah I'll still do that. Look if people want me, feels sort of... rude... to turn them down, y'know?

THE BUZZ - *A play by Lydia Rynne*

KYLA   Yeah, tell me about it! My arms are aching from batting away all my adoring fans!

She turns around to see he's gone. She's talking to herself...

KYLA   *(shouting after him)* And my feminist cage is not Rusty!

She laughs. But her smile gradually fades. She spots a bottle of wine hidden behind a fake cactus, fills a glass in the kitchen. She raises it, a toast to herself.

KYLA   To Kyla Squires, 2016 TV Personality of The Year!

She takes a long gulp of wine then raises her glass again.

KYLA   To Kyla...whatever her surname is.. 2018 Nobody of the Year!

She drinks again, then reclines back on the sofa. After a few moments she finds the remote and turns the volume up on the TV. We can hear the TV interview.

INTERVIEWER   And the next 'Twestion' we have for Mila, live tweeted to us this very moment, is from BigBunz87, who wants to ask Mila, 'your hair is well fit?' Not really a question there BigBunz but we have to agree that Mila's new haircut is awesome! And last but not least, our final Twestion comes from ZackFanBoy93, who asks 'are you fat cos Zack dumped you or are you...just.... fat - ... Okay, we're gunna wrap up right there, thank you SO much Mila for joining us here at See-leb, 'your first stop for all the hottest celeb goss'. Next up, guess who Panda's getting up close with in the studio -

KYLA   A stick of bamboo?!

INTERVIEWER   THE Joshua Franklyn! Did your heart just skip a beat? Mine did!

Upbeat techno music on TV as Kyla tops up her drink in the kitchen.

14

THE BUZZ - A play by Lydia Rynne

PANDA on TV   Joshua.. Thanks so much for joining us on the sofa today.

JOSH on TV   It's awesome to be here!

Screams from the young studio audience.

PANDA on TV   Before we move onto the twestions, can I just say - I personally LOVE your song lyrics, they're just so... relatable. How do you come up with them?

As he answers, Kyla continues drinking, numbly, watching the TV.

JOSH on TV   Cheers Panda.. I mean, I know a lot of musicians who have to take themselves away to the countryside or something crazy to get properly, you know, in the zone. I mean, I don't know whether it's a blessing or a curse, but for me, the lyrics just won't stop coming, it's like I can't close the floodgates -

PANDA on TV   Well everyone here at See-leb hopes those floodgates stay open for as long as possible!

JOSH on TV   As long as water's flowing, then so is Joshua Franklyn!

KYLA grabs the remote, switches the TV off and chucks the remote away from her, like it's diseased. She paces around the lounge.

KYLA   Sounds like diarrhea.

The buzzer to the flat sounds, Kyla looks towards the door. It sounds again. She picks up the entry phone suspiciously.

KYLA   Hello?.... Nate?! What the hell are you - wait are there any hacks out there? Look behind you, in the bushes - yeah I know it sounds cliched but that really is where they hide - you're sure?

She buzzes him up. She is in shock. Adjusts her hair, her clothes. There's a gentle knock on the front door. Before opening, she takes a deep breath, then slides the latch open. NATE enters and throws his arms around her. She looks uncomfortable.

NATE			I've missed you so much! Ooh, is this going? I am gasping!

He swoops the wine bottle off the side counter, swigs from it and closes his eyes and holds it up in appreciation.

NATE			Mmmm, I'm getting hints of... mum's stewed plums... Wet dog and...what is it? That's it, cowshit! Yup, tastes like home!

He walks around the apartment taking it in. She watches him with caution as if he's a wild animal.

NATE			Where's Josh then?

KYLA			Oh he's in bed.

NATE			*(whispered)* Whoops, sorry..

KYLA			It's okay, we got the walls sound-proofed so -

NATE			You can have crazy sex?

KYLA			No, he, Josh needs his sleep, and I stay up late, or later so -

NATE			Must be in the blood, I'm the same. All my thoughts seem to come at night... God it's white in here isn't it? Reminds me of a spaceship.

KYLA			Apparently white makes it look bigger.. We paid some spotty interior design grad three grand to tell us that.

NATE			I've been looking for you on the telly Ky.

KYLA			You're wasting your time there. Those days are well and truly behind me.

NATE   You're better without all that anyway I reckon. Success turns smart people crazy. Like smack, it'll never be enough, only leave you gurning for more.

She takes the bottle from him, fills her own glass and takes a gulp. He watches her with concern.

NATE   You're on edge.

KYLA   Very observant Nate.

NATE   But why?

KYLA   Maybe it's cos I haven't seen you in, what, eighteen months then you rock up in the middle of the night, unannounced. Someone could've seen you come in, taken a photo then it'll be online tomorrow, 'Joshua Franklyn linked to anarchist'.

NATE   You're an anarchist now? Nice one sis!

Nate grins and flops down onto the sofa and taps the space next to him. Kyla considers but stays standing.

KYLA   I can't stay up for long, we've got a shoot tomorrow.

NATE   We?

KYLA   I'm Josh's publicist now. Since I had the time, so -

NATE   Woah, that must be a bit weird?

KYLA   No - why would it be weird?

NATE   Working for your boyfriend.

KYLA   Not for. *With.*

Beat

| NATE | Well at least have one drink with me or you gunna just stand there?.... You won't sleep yet anyway, it's only one o'clock. |

He's right. So Kyla relents and sits down.

| NATE | So, how have you *really* been? |//
| KYLA | Yeah we're awesome, this last year his profile's skyrocketed, I've got to show you the photos. |

She takes out her phone but he ignores it.

| NATE | You should try doing open-mic nights again, like you did back home. |//
| KYLA | So this one's from the Europe tour last year - |

She tries to show him the photos on the phone. But he refuses to look at it, looking directly at her.

| NATE | Why not? |//
| KYLA | What? |//
| NATE | Open mics. You have a beautiful voice, you write beautiful songs. |

She gives up and puts her phone down.

| KYLA | I'm starting this blog. |//
| NATE | What like pictures of your breakfast? |//
| KYLA | More like lifestyle stuff. Fashion, exercise.. |//
| NATE | But you hate fashion. And exercise! |//
| KYLA | Shut-up, no I don't. |

THE BUZZ - *A play by Lydia Rynne*

NATE	Said you would wear a bin bag if it was socially acceptable so you could eat what you wanted and not care about it spilling down any fancy clothes!
KYLA	Well I don't remember saying that.
NATE	Well you did.
KYLA	Well I guess I've grown up.

Beat

KYLA	So enough grilling me - what about you? You look happy?
NATE	Yeah? And what does happiness look like?
KYLA	Don't be a dick.
NATE	Sorry. You're right, I am happy... Happ*ier*, anyways. Then that's not hard is it, there's not much more soul destroying than changing your own mum's nappies as she asks who you are and what the hell you're doing in her house!

He laughs and drinks. Kyla nods, the penny's dropped.

KYLA	So that's why you're here, I've been waiting for this.
NATE	For what?
KYLA	I knew you blamed me.
NATE	What are you on about Ky?
KYLA	You didn't have to stay after mum died, you could've left.
NATE	Yeah I know I could -
KYLA	I mean anyone's bound to get depressed in Chorley.

NATE	But I don't live in Chorley. I live here, in London.
KYLA	Alright then, whereabouts?
NATE	Just down the road, behind Currys.
KYLA	Behind Currys?
NATE	It's this electrical appliance shop -
KYLA	I know what Currys is Nate, Jesus I don't live under a rock... How long have you been there?
NATE	A few months, maybe a year, it's this communal living space, in an old Woolworth's. We call it Base.
KYLA	Oh my god, you live in a squat?!
NATE	There's like twenty of us now - artists, campaigners -
KYLA	- stoners, dropouts?
NATE	They're actually well cool Ky-
KYLA	I can't believe you've been living down the road all this time and never told me! I thought you might be dead.. Or in prison.. or at least in a cult!
NATE	Did you look for me?
KYLA	I sent you messages.
NATE	In the post?
KYLA	Yeah in the post, Nate, by owl mail! No, we're in the twenty first century FYI so I did what normal people do, I text you, tweeted you, tried to find you on facebook -
NATE	I don't have a phone or a telly or a laptop. Gave them away. Don't even have a watch now, swapped it for a prawn sandwich at a protest.

THE BUZZ - *A play by Lydia Rynne*

She stares at him in disbelief. He absentmindedly strokes a black fluffy cushion.

NATE		What's this made of, badger?

KYLA		Do you actually care or are you taking the piss?

NATE		Taking the piss.

KYLA		I know this isn't your world, Nate, but it is mine -

NATE		Is it?

KYLA		Yes! So you can go and tell all of your squat pals that I didn't sell out, I wanted this life, I worked for it.

NATE		And I'm proud of you, honest. I've told everyone down at Base about you. I tell them you inspired me to fight for what I believe in. Taught me to 'reach for the stars'.

KYLA		That's just an S-Club-7 song.

NATE		You had it painted on your bedroom wall, in blood!

KYLA		It was red paint, but I'm glad it inspired you.

NATE		You knew what you wanted and you never stopped trying did ya? And now here you are, in the spaceship of dreams.

Nate looks up at the massive poster of Josh on the wall.

NATE		His speech was well long wasn't it?

KYLA		Thought you didn't have a telly.

NATE   We watch it through the windows down at Curry's. It's
             well funny trying to guess what they might be saying-
             like the people on the telly are puppets and we're
             ventriloquists. Remember when we used to play that?
             You'd do the voice and I'd do the faces on my hands?
             Mum loved that, didn't she? Pissed herself laughing -

KYLA   I don't remember that, no. Listen, Nate, as nice as
             this is, I'm getting tired, we've got this shoot
             tomorrow -

NATE   *Josh* has a shoot, you don't. I'm your little brother
             Ky. Stay up with me for a bit yeah? You're going out
             with a rockstar - what happened to live fast die young?

KYLA   Yeah, it's not like that these days. Kate Moss and Pete
             Docherty stumbling out of clubs like Bambi trying to
             walk on ice isn't what gets people going. Now they want
             their role models healthy, wholesome ... reliable.

NATE   Like a loaf of granary bread.

KYLA   Exactly.

NATE   Please? One more drink?

Kyla considers.

KYLA   And you're sure you haven't come to entice me into this
             cult of yours?

NATE   Do you want me to?

KYLA   Can you imagine me in somewhere like that? The last
             time I slept rough I was in a bell tent with a fridge
             full of chilled wine and the bed had massage settings.
             Alexa Chung's tent was opposite mine and I swear I
             heard Tom and Taylor orgasm in the yurt next door...

She looks at Nate wanting a response at these name drops. Nothing...

NATE   Am I supposed to know who these people are?

THE BUZZ - *A play by Lydia Rynne*

KYLA   Oh my god - what planet are you from?!

NATE   Same planet as you! (*he puts on an alien/ET voice*) And I've come to bring you home!

He makes the sound of a rocket taking off into the sky. Kyla shakes her head at him but lets herself laugh for the first time since he's arrived.

KYLA   You're a nutter. But I've missed you. Does that make me a nutter too?

He grins back at her and she hugs him, desperately.

Later. A half empty tequila bottle is on the table - they're on their way to drunk. Nate is strumming on a guitar the chords for Tracy Chapman's 'Talkin' About a Revolution', nodding at Kyla urging her to join in. She does so, at first nervously, but growing in confidence - she has a good voice. They sing the chorus together and lie back on the sofa laughing.

NATE   When did people stop writing songs that actually mean something? So bored of love and heartbreak like that's the only thing that matters. Give me a song about real shit you know? About all those kids being washed up on our shores like driftwood, about the fact we're ruining the universe just by existing, about political corruption. About all these rich fuckers burying their money in the Bermuda triangle.

KYLA   Do it then! Write the songs, sing them loud and clear. If you don't some other fucker will only go and do it first.

NATE   Alright, I will. Maybe Josh can hook us up with his contacts, get us a deal. Me on guitar, you on vocals -

KYLA   No way, I've lost my voice. Too many -

NATE   Blowjobs?

KYLA | Eurgh, almost as bad as when mum said scissoring. 'Mind yourselves little'uns, I'm scissoring the lamb chops!'

They crack up laughing again.

NATE | Seriously, you have got to come to Base some time, you'd fit right in.

KYLA | Isn't it all 'dude', dreadlocks and saving the world one spliff at a time?

NATE | Something like that...

Kyla looks melancholic.

KYLA | Maybe I could get used to doing this every day. I'm bored out of my mind up here, so may as well use the time to dream and sing about a revolution that'll never happen!

NATE | Don't say it won't happen, cos it could. It will. Trust me. What goes up has to come down... The people at the top, they can't stay there forever. It's like mother nature. Everything that lives must die...

Kyla pouts at him, patronisingly, pinches his cheek.

KYLA | Awww, you really are in your twenties aren't you?

NATE | I'm serious! They're all proper clever the guys I live with. A lot of them are campaigners, you know for charities and stuff. This guy Beardy's even starting up his own party.

KYLA | We go to boring parties. Full of skinny rats with empty stomachs and emptier heads.

NATE | - I meant like political parties... I'm helping make the poster for the one Beardy's pulling together. It's gunna be called 'Us'. Cos it's about the collective, not the individual.

KYLA   You're an individual.

NATE   No I'm not.

Kyla starts laughing, he struggles to make his point over her laughter.

NATE   At least, I'm trying not to be.

KYLA   You sound like such a massive stoner!

NATE   It's actually really fucking dangerous this cult of the individual -

She can't stop laughing.

KYLA   Cult of the Individual! Woooooooh spooky!

NATE   A hundred years ago, we did stuff for the sake of the community -

KYLA   Well, this is my kinda community: me, you and a bottle of..... Oh no... Emergency!!

She looks sadly into the empty wine bottle, then into the tequila bottle and makes a siren sound of an ambulance.

NATE   You have to listen to me, it's really important!

KYLA   Nate love, if I'd wanted a history lesson, I'd read a book. But right now, in 2018, we've run out of le alcohol...

NATE   But that's just it! When *did* you last read a book? No-one reads anymore. And I don't mean some wanker's lifestyle blog on your laptop. I mean a book about ideas... Ideas that could change the world. Have you read the Communist Manifesto?

KYLA   Jesus, you really have joined a cult haven't you.

NATE	How is wanting to change the world for the better culty?! You used to love talking about this stuff, about how we need to stick it to the man. You took me to my first protest, we got the Megabus before dawn, it was amazing, we were right on the front line, together -
KYLA	And then I grew up!
NATE	Or *gave* up?

Kyla considers this for a split second before her phone buzzes. She looks at it and keeps her eyes on it, tapping away, during the below.

NATE	Did you know Mrs Ayres died?... Ky?
KYLA	Hmmm?
NATE	Mrs Ayres?
KYLA	What about her?
NATE	She died. From loneliness.

Kyla looks up, with a smirk.

KYLA	Shut-up.
NATE	I'm serious. Her kids flew the nest, one of them to Australia, the other to Luton, then a month later, she was dead in her bed. The doctors couldn't find a physical cause so they think her body and mind just gave up. That's how important it is - community, family, holding onto the things that matter -
KYLA	No-one told me.
NATE	About what?
KYLA	The funeral. You should've told me.
NATE	Would've you come?

She shrugs as she looks back at her phone.

NATE   The cottage is still full of stuff, stuff we need to sort through.

KYLA   Can't we just pay some blokes to take it to a dump? That's a thing right? There's probably an app...

Nate stares at her in disbelief. She finishes on her phone and eventually puts it down, notices Nate's expression.

KYLA   What?!

NATE   This is all we have left of our childhood, of our mum...

KYLA   Alright, alright, we'll go there... Just not yet.

NATE   Why?

KYLA   Josh has - *we* have a lot lined up.

NATE   He doesn't even... Nevermind...

KYLA   What? Say it?

NATE   He doesn't appreciate you. Not like you deserve anyway.

She picks up her phone again.

NATE   Look at me.

KYLA   Gimme a minute - Twitter's blowing up after tonight.

NATE   He's done this to you.

KYLA   Oh my god, Aaron X looks like a absolute twat!

She tries to show Nate but he turns away from her, irritated.

NATE   I think it would be good for us to go back, together. We can properly say goodbye to mum's cottage -

She is chuckling at something on her screen, completely absorbed. Nate takes it from her hands, drops it on the floor and stamps on it. She stares at him in disbelief.

KYLA   What the fuck is wrong with you?!

NATE   You weren't listening to me!

KYLA   You're insane, you're actually insane.

She kneels to pick up the pieces.

NATE   I just - I hate seeing you like this!

KYLA   I knew it was a mistake letting you in, so fucking immature -

NATE   *Me* immature?! You're the one scrabbling around on the floor like you're piecing together a broken body. It's a PHONE Kyla. I don't even have one.

KYLA   What part of being Josh's *publicist* are you not getting? Now how am I going to tweet at tomorrow's shoot?

NATE   Look I buy weed off one of the guys at Curry's, so I'll fix it for you tomorrow. But for now, why not see it as a night off from technology. A night to focus on what's right in front of you...

She gives up picking up the pieces and sits on the sofa next to him. After a few seconds of silence, Nate nods at the poster of Josh.

NATE   God he's a handsome bugger isn't he?

Kyla shrugs a little.

NATE   The face that launched a thousand records. Must have a fair bit of cash saved up by now ey?-

She stands up, blocks Nate's view of the Josh poster.

THE BUZZ - *A play by Lydia Rynne*

KYLA   Alright here's the deal. You want to stay here tonight, we don't talk about him again. Understood? You're my brother, I want your full attention.

NATE   Fine by me.

KYLA   Good.

NATE   One problem.

Nate is looking in the drinks cabinet - everything is empty.

NATE   I think we're going to need more booze...

Kyla nods, determined.

Nate, alone in the flat, is looking out of the window, nervously. There is a knock on the front door and he rushes to it. He fumbles with the door locks and lets in ANON wearing a horse mask.

ANON   Where's she gone?

NATE   Gone to get more booze - what's with the mask?

ANON   Just don't, alright? Amazon's stopped selling the normal anarchy one - can barely see a thing - Jesus it's white in here. So, where's the star of the show?

NATE   Sleeping I think.

ANON   Which room?

NATE   Errr that one. No wait, maybe that one -

ANON   You've been here an hour and you haven't done a reccy?

NATE   A what?

ANON   I thought you were into this!?

29

THE BUZZ - A play by Lydia Rynne

Anon looks at the empty bottles littering the table, the guitar.

ANON   Instead you glug your way through her drinks cabinet while I'm waiting outside in a bush covered in pigeon shit.

NATE   Listen, I don't know how I feel about all this Cordelia

ANON   Anon!

NATE   Anon, whatever... I just... is this the best way?

In the wind, the front door slams shut behind them, startling them both. Josh calls for Kyla from the bedroom. Anon signals for Nate to turn off the lights. He tries to, but as it's a touch sensitive light, it just dims a bit then goes even brighter. She shoves Nate aside brusquely and turns them off completely.

ANON   Now hide!

The bedroom door opens and we see Josh's silhouette in the doorway.

JOSH   Kyla can you call Jethro, tell him to come at nine not eight, I think I'll hit the gym first, tighten up before the shoot.... Baby?

He switches on the light, and Anon launches herself at him, with a roar and jabs him with what looks like a pen, several times on his bare arm. Josh staggers for a moment before collapsing onto the floor.

ANON   Yeah cheers for your help there Nate.

NATE   What was that... thing... that -

ANON   Ketamine -

NATE   You tranquilised him?!

ANON   He'll be having a lovely time, now we need to move fast -

NATE   He might be a dick but he's still my sister's boyfriend, you can't just stab my sister's boyfriend -

But Anon is dragging a sedated, groaning Josh over to the sofa.

NATE	Something about this doesn't feel right...

ANON	Maybe the fact that this talentless cunt isn't paying his taxes? Now are you going to help me teach him a lesson or what?

Nate hesitates, before joining Anon in tying Josh's hands and feet together and placing gaffer tape over his mouth.

Anon takes out a small flip cam, passes it to Nate, pulls her horse mask on again and shakes Josh awake. He opens his eyes, takes in the horse face and tries to stand up but, his feet still tied together, and heavily drugged, he falls back down again onto the sofa.

ANON	Are you getting all this Nate? I want you right up here in his face.

She turns her attention back to Josh.

ANON	Morning Joshua! Thanks for joining us here on the couch. How you doing today?

Josh starts crying, delirious.

ANON	Oh wow, this is goldust.

NATE	Cordelia can we please just -

ANON	ANON!

NATE	Whatever, look I really don't think we should upset him any more, Kyla's gunna come back, and I thought the main thing was just getting an admission, then leaving -

ANON	If you don't like it, go, there's no way I'm wasting this kind of opportunity.

Nate gives up and carries on filming, but looking out of the window every so often nervously. Anon puts on an interviewers voice.

Anon turns to the camera, forcing Josh's face towards it.

ANON   Morning kids, today we're doing a special called The Rich and Shameless! First up we have someone you should recognise -

NATE   Please hurry up!!

ANON   - the one, the only, Joooooshua Franklyn! *(she makes an applauding noise)* So, without further ado, question numero uno, do you give a shit about anyone but yourself?

Anon makes Josh's head shake from side to side.

ANON   Did you catch that folks, Joshua does NOT, I repeat NOT give a shit about anyone else, not you, his fans, and definitely, definitely not me...

Nate has spotted Kyla outside.

NATE   Shit she's back!

ANON   Can you go and stall her?! I'm not done yet!

Nate leaves the camera on the table, and exits, leaving the door to the flat open behind him. When he's gone Anon rushes to shut the door behind him, takes her horse mask off, and shakes Josh awake again.

ANON   Hey, wake up. Remember me? Oi, I said REMEMBER ME?! Hotel Sapphire, May last year? No? Wow, you sure know how to make a girl feel special..

He tries to speak from under the gaffer tape.

ANON   Sorry I can't hear you? Can you say that again?

He tries to speak again.

ANON	Nope, afraid I didn't catch that either? You said you DO want me to film you? You DO want this to go online?

He starts trying to stand, panicked, but can't, stumbling back.

ANON	Don't worry, I'm not going to hurt you. Not physically anyway... All kinds of things flashed through my mind before coming here, dark things, brutal things, things I didn't think I was capable of imagining -

Josh tries to shout for Kyla from behind the gaffer tape.

ANON	Oh she's not here. It's just us. Just like it was that night. Now, I know you were brought up catholic - you've got that lovely Topman range of rosary beads, so I want a confession, like the good catholic boy you are-

At this moment Nate enters and signals frantically for Anon to hide. Anon quickly jabs Josh again in the arm with the ketamine injection and he slumps forward. She ducks behind the sofa. Kyla enters mid-conversation, and continues into the kitchen, plonking her purchases down on the breakfast bar, unaware of Josh on the sofa.

KYLA	- So in the end I got red and white but no rose cos I'm sorry but it isn't a wine it's a juice drink for children, Josh's favourite of course.

She starts pouring two glasses of red.

KYLA	You know it stains your teeth big time? One glass is like ten coffees in one go it's so bad. I don't give a shit but Josh tells me this stuff, got a head full of all these pointless facts about your teeth or skin or even cuticles. I mean who knew people gave a crap about the flap of skin that joins your fingers to your nails?

Josh groans from behind the gaffer tape, and Kyla sees him on the sofa, looking up at her desperately. She looks to Nate, surprisingly calm.

KYLA	What's going on?

NATE   Yeah so it's sort of a weird story -

KYLA   Untie him before I phone the police.

NATE   Just sit down, I've got something to tell you -

KYLA   I said - untie him.

ANON stands up from behind the sofa, with her horse mask on.

ANON   I'm sorry but I'm not finished yet.

Kyla looks at Nate again.

KYLA   Who the fuck is this -

NATE   This is Cordelia -

ANON   Anon, it's short for Anonymous.

KYLA   Jesus christ...

Kyla walks towards Josh, but Nate blocks her.

KYLA   Move.

NATE   She's my friend, from Base.

KYLA   Yeah I guessed that.

She tries to move past him again, but he holds her by the shoulders.

KYLA   Is he drugged?

NATE   What? No -

ANON   Ketamine, not much though -

KYLA   If I wasn't pissed, I'd strangle you Nate. I only see you once in a blue moon, and boy do you make sure it's memorable.

She laughs in disbelief, as if she's in a dream.

NATE	This is serious Ky, we've got to tell you something -

KYLA	That you're into bondage? Good for you! Now fuck off!

ANON	I'm not leaving now, no way -

Kyla goes into the bedroom and comes out with Josh's phone.

NATE	What are you doing?

KYLA	Phoning the police.

NATE	Oh god, we've done this all wrong, we've scared you..

KYLA	Oh no, you didn't.

NATE	Upset you then -

KYLA	I went numb years ago Nate, nothing surprises me anymore.

NATE	It's just - well- Cordelia's dad works for this... like... what is it?

ANON	Leave it Nate.

NATE	What? No. This is... Listen, he's a banker, or accountant or something like that, and he got hold of this stuff, on Josh. On something secret, something bad. So we came here to tell you, to make sure you knew the type of person you were living with.

Kyla starts to laugh. Nate looks perturbed, at Cordelia.

NATE	This is serious Ky, Cordelia's dug up some serious dirt -

KYLA	Yeah? And how much are the magazines paying her for this 'dirt'?

THE BUZZ - *A play by Lydia Rynne*

ANON   I'm right here...

KYLA   In my flat. Uninvited. So you are. I knew you were naive Nate, but this is really pathetic...

She starts to dial, but he grabs it off her.

NATE   Stop talking to me like that!

KYLA   Like what?!

NATE   Like you don't trust me. I'm your brother. Your only family and you won't even listen.

She looks up at him, gives him the floor.

KYLA   Go on then.. Tell me.

NATE   I didn't believe it at first, I like Josh, sort of, on a basic level, you know I do, well I did. After what he did for me, after the protest and the bail and that... But when it comes to injustice, I just can't stand it Ky, you know like they say in books and stuff when someone 'sees red', well when she told me -

ANON   Nate stop -

NATE   She deserves to know the truth -

ANON   Please let me speak -

NATE   She's my sister!!

Anon goes quiet.

NATE   Josh has been using a tax dodging scheme, Ky.

Disappointed in her lack of reaction he tries again.

NATE   For years, ever since he became big three years ago

ANON   It's not true.

THE BUZZ - *A play by Lydia Rynne*

NATE   He - *(he turns to Anon)* What did you say.. ?

ANON   The papers, the tax dodging...I made it up.

NATE   Don't get scared now, we're doing the right thing. Kyla, you should know, Josh has been investing in offshore accounts... He's tried to keep it separate from you. he's been putting away millions and millions, all while being the face of fucking Shepherd's Watch homeless charity! How twisted can you get?

ANON   No, he hasn't.

NATE   Yes, he has. She has to hear it Cordelia! She has a right to know who she lives with!

ANON   I'm telling you Nate I MADE IT UP!

NATE   But... what?

ANON   You were so keen, so eager to help, to be a part of something that mattered, you didn't even ask to see the papers?!

Nate looks ashamed. It's sinking in.

NATE   You're telling me that - that he - that my sister's boyfriend didn't do anything?

ANON   Nevermind..

KYLA   Right, that's it, party's over.

NATE   I don't understand...

Anon is suddenly scared, disorientated, panicked.

ANON   I shouldn't be here.

NATE   Are you a fan?!

THE BUZZ - *A play by Lydia Rynne*

ANON   What? No...

KYLA   Course she is -

NATE   Is that true?

KYLA   Why else would she be here -

ANON   I'M NOT A FAN!

Nate and Kyla both stop talking, stunned at the outburst.

NATE   Well what is it then?

ANON   I... It doesn't matter, let's go.

NATE   Cordelia?

ANON   He raped me.

Beat

ANON   He raped me. Last year -

KYLA   How much do you want?

She grabs her wallet.

KYLA   I don't carry cash, but here take my card - Nate go with her to the nearest ATM -

ANON   I'm sorry, I really am sorry -

KYLA   And I feel sorry for you, I really do -

NATE   Wait, what's happening here?

KYLA   You've been used is what's happening - your pal here is probably trying to sell a story - got a student loan to cover do you?

ANON   Please, I'm being serious -

KYLA	So am I - now get out of my apartment.

Nate looks at Anon, upset.

NATE	You used me.
ANON	No, that's not it -
NATE	He's practically family for fuck's sake!
ANON	I know... Which is why she deserves to know
KYLA	A grand? Two? Alright fine, five?
ANON	They've already paid me off ten grand to shut up and disappear.
NATE	I can't believe I fell for this bullshit. I'm so sorry, Kyla.

He takes Anon by the arm and tries to drag her to the door, but just as they get there Kyla speaks.

KYLA	Who paid you?
NATE	What?
KYLA	I'm talking to your friend. Ten thousand, who -
ANON	I forget the names, his people... Think AJ, or PJ -
KYLA	KJ.
ANON	That's it. I didn't meet him. He sent some driver-
KYLA	Jethro.
ANON	Maybe. I don't know... I was a mess, on my way to rehab.
NATE	You can't just say stuff like that Cordelia.

THE BUZZ - *A play by Lydia Rynne*

ANON	It's true.
KYLA	When was this?

Kyla walks over to the counter to get herself a drink.

ANON	May 26th. Last year.
KYLA	Where?
ANON	Blue Sapphire hotel. It's this fancy, five star place...
KYLA	I know, I booked it for him.
NATE	Wait, so this is actually real? This actually happened?
KYLA	And what happened?
ANON	Which part -
KYLA	All of it, from the start..
ANON	All of it?
KYLA	That's what I said.

She nods at Anon to continue. She takes her time.

ANON	Okay. So. Well, we met in the hotel bar. He had all these interviews, I was interning for the tour company. I'd never been to a five star hotel before - was sort of wrapped up in it all. Sending selfies to my mates back home and stuff -
KYLA	Okay maybe not from the start, fast forward -
ANON	Um, okay, and then suddenly it was just me and him left. And he asked if I wanted to hear his new album. Live. I said yes. Cos what else could you say? Joshua Franklyn asks you something like that - He said he wanted his fans to -

THE BUZZ - *A play by Lydia Rynne*

KYLA   To see the real him?

ANON   Yeah, that's it.

NATE   Can I just check what's happening here...?

KYLA   No. *(she turns to Anon)* Keep going.

NATE   I'm just scared that this is, like, a *big* claim.

KYLA   So sit down and shut-up. *(turning to Anon again)* So you went to his room and -?

Finally given the floor, Anon looks overwhelmed, nervous.

ANON   I'm sorry, I regret it now, obviously

KYLA   I'm not angry. Not with you. Carry on..

ANON   I was drunk, but I was still *there,* you know, mentally. And we were just kissing and that. With my clothes on. At first. I'm pretty shy usually - I hate telling you this - you're probably a really nice person -

KYLA   I'm not, don't worry.

ANON   Right.. So um. He was trying to put his hands down, you know - there - but once I set my mind against something, I don't change it easily. I've always been like that... So I told him, I said not tonight, I said it nicely. And, I guess I felt a bit....ungrateful? Cos I knew at the time, I remember thinking - God, there must be a million girls, and guys, that would kill to be in my position right here in Joshua Franklyn's arms, but I did say no - should I stop now?

NATE   This is insane. I have no clue what's happening -

KYLA   Carry on.

ANON   Well that's sort of... it.

KYLA   Full sex?

Anon nods apologetically

KYLA   Did you tell anyone?

ANON   Just my mum. And a mate. But they haven't said anything

KYLA   You didn't go to the police?

ANON   I didn't think there was any point!

Kyla starts pacing around the room, thinking.

ANON   Some fangirl goes to Josh Franklyn's hotel room to 'listen to records'? I'm asking for it, right? I didn't have any bruises or scratches or the kind of things the girls on the TV shows have after they've .... after it's happened to them... Weirdly it was sort of... gentle.

NATE   Gentle?! That doesn't sound like rape!?

Anon looks panicked, doubting herself.

ANON   But - but - the point is I didn't want it! I said that loud and clear, but you know when you're in a popstar's room, and they've been playing you music and giving you drinks and telling you you can come on tour with them. The way he was looking at me, it was like he thought he was god, you know? And I guess God gets his way..

KYLA   Only if you believe in him...

ANON   Well maybe I'm weak, but after a while I just sort of... Gave in..

NATE   You 'gave in'?

ANON   Or gave up...? I don't know...

NATE   This is ridiculous.

Anon begins to cry. She looks exhausted as she slumps down onto the floor. Kyla hugs her. Josh starts to come around on the sofa, disorientated.

KYLA   You should leave now. I'll handle it.

ANON   But, wait, what will you do?

KYLA   Just, trust me, okay?

She goes and opens the front door, for them to leave.

ANON   I'm really sorry.

KYLA   This isn't your fault.

NATE   I can't leave you here with him.

KYLA   I've been left him with him for the last three years.

NATE   Why don't you come with us?

KYLA   There's things I need to sort first...

Nate hugs Kyla, then leaves with Anon.

Kyla closes the door. She takes the gaffer out of Josh's mouth. Then, on seeing Anon's horse mask left on the floor, puts it on, picks up a glass of wine and chucks it in Josh's face. He opens his eyes and flinches away from her, scared, thinking she's Anon, slurring and disorientated still.

JOSH   What're you... What do you want from me?... Apology? Money? ... Where's Kyla? KYLA?!!... Fuckssakes you wanted it too - I know you did... KYLA!!!... You came to MY room remember... Why do that if you don't want to go through with it? You a prick tease? Is that it? .... KYLA?! Where is fucking Kyla?

Kyla walks out the front door. After a few moments of Josh trying to pull himself out of the ropes, Kyla re-enters, without the horse mask on, all smiles.

KYLA   She's fucking here, what's up?

JOSH   Kyla - Kyla baby - oh my god I missed you - this crazy Fan was here, your nutter brother let them in - I told you he can't be trusted didn't I? Would you fucking untie these things?

KYLA   Ummmm... Nahhh.

JOSH   You what?

KYLA   I said 'NAH'.

Josh laughs, nervously.

JOSH   Baby, don't mess me around, we need to phone the police, then I need my sleep for tomorrow's shoot-

KYLA   There isn't going to be a shoot.

JOSH   What?

KYLA   It's been cancelled. KJ called.

JOSH   When? Why would he call you?

KYLA   You were tied up taking ketamine on the coach.

JOSH   What... What's happened...?

KYLA   I met an old acquaintance of yours.

JOSH   You were here? You were here while the crazy fan girl basically *tortured* me?

KYLA   I wouldn't exactly call her a fan, Josh... She told me what you did.

JOSH	I'm so confused...
KYLA	Yeah and it sounds like you were confused that night too. Between the words 'yes' and 'no'.
JOSH	What!?
KYLA	Blue Sapphire. Penthouse suite - 'room with a view' just like you asked baby.
JOSH	I have no clue who she is. Why would you believe someone like *her* over -
KYLA	Someone like *you*?! You don't even write the songs you sell! I do! And what thanks do I get? Fuck all!
JOSH	Why are you doing this? Don't you enjoy our life?

Kyla bursts out laughing.

KYLA	What about this could ever be 'enjoyable' for me?! I float around up here in this fucking... cloud... waiting for you to come home so I soak up a smidgen of your success - that's not living, that's not even surviving.
JOSH	I never... I didn't know you were so unhappy.
KYLA	You never asked.
JOSH	You should've said.
KYLA	And what would've you done about it? Another massage? Another spa retreat for one? I'm an intelligent person Josh. But to everyone out there, I'm the dress hanging off your arm. And they don't even like the dress I'm wearing enough to print it in the papers... That's not good enough for me. Not anymore.
JOSH	But... But what about the album?
KYLA	I've been asking about it for months, but you never have the time.

JOSH	I know I've had my head in the clouds for the last few months, but things will calm down after the tour... Only if you've got ideas though, otherwise we can push it back -
KYLA	I do have ideas. Loads of them. But, wait, this isn't real... is it?
JOSH	Why not?
KYLA	And you'd...You'd credit me?
JOSH	On the front cover. Where you deserve to be... I'm fed up of KJ and that telling me what's what. They'd be nothing without my music. Our music. So I'll call them tomorrow and tell them our plan.
KYLA	Are you - wait, are you pissing around? Cos it's not funny -
JOSH	Baby I swear on my mum's life. On my life. Now will you untie me?
KYLA	First, I need you to tell me the truth.
JOSH	Course.
KYLA	Did you do what - what she said? Did you rape that woman?

Josh laughs in disbelief.

JOSH	Can you imagine me, raping someone?! I can barely write a song on my own without freaking out, how am I going to go through with something like that? Look, maybe I've flirted with a few girls in the past, played them some songs, hey this was in my first year of being famous - course I'd wanna bask in the glory a little bit. But rape?! Fuck that... Now will you *please* untie me?

Kyla thinks for a moment, before kneeling down and beginning to untie him. Lights down.

A few days later, Kyla is sitting on the sofa. She looks different. Calm. She dials a number on her phone.

KYLA   Hi it's me. Yep, we're ready to go.

Josh comes in from the bedroom, dressed to go out, shades on, a cap. Kyla quickly hangs up.

KYLA   All packed?

JOSH   Yup. America here we come!

KYLA   You. Not we...

JOSH   Yeah I'm sorry about that babe. KJ just gets funny about girls coming on tour, in case we get, like, distracted, you know?

KYLA   Unless it's Katie.

JOSH   But that's different, she's my publicist.

KYLA   Is she better than me?

JOSH   She knows how to Instagram. Your big thumbs kept putting the 'and' sign instead of hashtag. Pretty big difference. Call Jethro and tell him I'll be down in five will ya?

Josh sets about making himself a juice.

KYLA   Has KJ set any recording dates for when you're back?

JOSH   You what?

KYLA   You said you'd talk to him about us, our album?

JOSH	Ah yeah, bit of a shitter, turns out the tour might be longer than we expected..
KYLA	Till August you said?
JOSH	Yeah that's right, but it's really going to take it out of me. So KJ reckons it's probably best we save that whole album thing till after everything's calmed down.
KYLA	Calmed down.
JOSH	You know after the next tour or whatever. You have to think about it from a business perspective babe. I'm the face of a massive brand -
KYLA	And I put the words in your massive mouth.

He laughs and ruffles her hair.

JOSH	You're my rock, you know that? You know what I think we could do with, when I'm back, let's go away somewhere, out of the city, just the two of us, somewhere no-one can find us, not even the paps, you can top up your tan, course I'll already be pretty tanned from California, but I reckon it'll be good for you to have something to look forward to, something to focus on while I'm away.

Kyla isn't listening, she is in her own world. She laughs to herself, shaking her head in disbelief.

KYLA	All those words...

Josh looks uncertain now, tries to catch up.

JOSH	Yeah cos you're a major part of it babe, it's like everyone's done their little bit, like a chessboard yeah, and I'm like the king. But KJ and that, they're like God. And they've got all the next moves sorted, way before I even know. And all these moves need to be perfectly timed. So this is actually, weirdly, even though it might feel like it can't get any better, this is just the beginning for Joshua Franklyn! Ohhh shit, this top matches my shoes, I'm too matchy.

The buzzer sounds.

JOSH	Shit that'll be Jethro, be a babe and tell him I'll be another five yeah?

JOSH exits into the bedroom. KYLA calmly walks over to the entry phone and picks it up.

KYLA	Third floor, penthouse. He's in the bedroom.

She takes the front door off the latch, picks up a bathrobe, puts it on, and exits. We hear the sound of the shower turning on.
Josh comes out of the bedroom.

JOSH	Kyla babe did you hear me? I said tell Jethro I'll be down in five?

The lights of a police car outside, followed by the flashing lights of photographers and a crowd of people. A helicopter above. The press are descending upon him. Josh shields his face from the glare.

JOSH	Wait, what's going on? Kyla? KYLAAAAA?!

Blackout.

A few weeks later. Daylight fills the room. Kyla comes out of the bathroom toweling her hair dry. She turns the TV on, it's the same upbeat techno music from See-leb we heard at the start. She watches it while taking the poster of Josh off the wall and rolling it up. The buzzer sounds, she goes over to it, her eyes still on the TV as she presses the entry button. Nate enters, excited, but his smile falls when he sees Kyla and the state of the flat.

NATE   I've booked a van for half two - are you going to be Ready?... Ky?

Nate stands between Kyla and the TV. Kyla, irritated, tries to lean past him to continue watching, as Josh did at the start.

KYLA   Move, they're just about to show the red carpet...

NATE   But you were there! Why do you need to watch it?!

Fed up, he switches it off. She tries to grab the remote off him, but he puts it behind his back.

NATE   Are you coming home with me or not?

Kyla avoids his gaze and lifts up the laptop.

KYLA   I've changed, Nate.

NATE   Not this again...

KYLA   I'm serious, I can't go back to what I was, not now.

NATE   But I can help you!

KYLA   What if I don't want to be helped? What if this is what I want?

NATE   You live in a plastic spaceship!

KYLA   At least a spaceship can reach for the stars!?

Kyla winks and waits for a laugh, but Nate is devastated. He sits down.

NATE	You said you were tired of all this. You said 'success is a joke, without a punchline' - that stayed with me that one...
KYLA	What can I say, I'm a writer!

She looks at him, his head in his hands. She clearly feels bad.

KYLA	I'm sorry alright. I did think I could go back. I did... This whole thing did make me miss the humdrum of normality. For a bit.. But now it's all over I -

Nate looks up in shock.

NATE	Over?! Cordelia had a breakdown Kyla! It's worse now than it was before. She's been chased through the streets by Josh's crazy fans, who blame her for ruining his career!
KYLA	And that's my fault because?
NATE	You should've told Cordelia what you were planning, before you phoned the papers.
KYLA	I wasn't 'planning' anything, and if I was it was for her benefit.
NATE	You don't have to lie - not to me.
KYLA	She came in here in a horse mask, tied him up and told me what he did to her. If that's not a cry for help I don't know what is.
NATE	You told her you'd sort it out. She believed you.
KYLA	And I did, didn't I?
NATE	You made it *your* story.

KYLA	It was her story for two years and no-one gave a shit! I used my profile so people would listen -and they did! That's why his career's over, that's why the world is now talking about him.
NATE	And you.
KYLA	What?
NATE	They're talking about you! When they should be talking about what happened to Cordelia, asking her how she feels. Not have you putting words in her mouth. Like a fucking puppet.
KYLA	Rich coming from you - you didn't even believe her to start with. Your were doing your best to shut her up.
NATE	And I regret that now...
KYLA	You seen her recently?

Nate shakes his head, sadly.

NATE	Base kicked her out from drawing too much attention to them... They're full of shit. Think they're fighting for something but then when there's the chance to stand up, they're frightened... or lazy... I don't know. That's why I'm leaving.
KYLA	So what'll you do, back home?
NATE	Figure out what's worth fighting for.
KYLA	I'll visit you sometime.
NATE	Liar.

She pecks him on the cheek. Nate nods sadly as she steps away from him, picks up the remote, turns the TV on. The See-Leb music strikes up. She walks into a spotlight. Nate's figure dims in the darkness of the stage behind her, and he leaves, sadly, closing the door behind him. We hear a V/O of the same interviewer's voice that we heard interviewing Josh on TV before.

INTERVIEWER   Kyla, thank you so much for joining us here on See-Leb!

KYLA   It's great to be here.

INTERVIEWER   Firstly, can I just say we are loving this new look -

KYLA   Thank you Panda, I'm not going to lie it hasn't been easy but the one bonus of the stress of this whole thing is I've dropped two dress sizes!

INTERVIEWER   Wow, what's your secret?

KYLA   Date a man who turns out to be a monster?!

INTERVIEWER   Which brings us onto - did you really have no idea about his past actions?

KYLA   He had a lot of secrets... Which is weird, since he was basically dependent on me for... well... certain other things!

INTERVIEWER   You mean the whole you writing the lyrics to all Joshua's songs and never once receiving a credit for them?

KYLA   I mean, sure, it sucks not to be credited for your work, but women are silenced in a lot more ways than that.. In the bedroom, in the media, in court... So I guess this album is for them really - the ones who have decided to speak up, but also for the ones who haven't. Cos you know, holding it all inside is just as hard.

THE BUZZ - A play by Lydia Rynne

INTERVIEWER   Well said Kyla, I'm looking forward to your Grammy's speech already! - And if you can't wait until November to get your mitts on the most anticipated album of the year, here's a sneak peek at what you can expect - do you want to do the honours Kyla.

KYLA   This is the title track from my debut album, 'My Time'. For all silenced women - let me hear you roar!

Upbeat pop music starts up. Kyla's smile fades as the spotlight also fades. She looks around her at the empty apartment, lost, scared. The music becomes distorted until all we can hear is the buzz of an untuned TV.

END

www.ingramcontent.com/pod-product-compliance
Lightning Source LLC
Chambersburg PA
CBHW071037080526
44587CB00015B/2662